The Masterpiece

The Masterpiece

STEVE BRADLEY

GLOBE FEARON
Pearson Learning Group

FASTBACK® HORROR BOOKS

All photography © Pearson Education, Inc. (PEI) unless specifically noted.

ISBN 0-13-024523-2

Printed in the United States of America

2 3 4 5 6 7 8 9 10   07 06 05

Globe Fearon

Pearson Learning Group

1-800-321-3106
www.pearsonlearning.com

Alan Carroll didn't know what it was, but he knew that something was wrong.

He looked carefully at the picture he had been painting. He looked at the open field and at the barn on one side of the field. He looked at the sky and at the clouds he had painted in that sky.

What's wrong with this picture? he asked himself. *It looks strange—wrong in some way. Is it too dark in here for me to paint well? Or is it that the colors I've used are the wrong ones?*

He went on looking at the picture, shaking his head, not able to answer his questions.

He picked up his palette on which there were many colors of paint. He dipped his brush into some paint that was the color of blood. He added some of the dark red to the sky in the picture. When he had done so, the sky looked stormy.

He shook his head again. *That's wrong,* he told himself. He picked up a cloth and wiped the paint from the canvas.

Something touched his knee.

He looked down and saw his dog, Boots, looking up at him. "I didn't know you were in here," he said and patted the dog's head.

Boots wagged his tail.

"Why can't I get any of my pictures to look right these days, Boots?" Alan asked, looking away from the dog to the painting resting on his easel.

Boots barked.

"I can't put my finger on just what's wrong," Alan said, more to himself than to Boots. "Well, I might as well call it a day."

He put down his palette and paint brush and then left the studio, with Boots right behind him.

He found his wife, Meg, sitting in the

kitchen. She was drinking a cup of coffee and staring blankly out the window.

"Hi, honey," Alan said.

Boots barked again.

Meg turned away from the window and pointed a finger at the dog. "Get that animal out of my kitchen? Now, Alan!"

"Why?" Alan asked.

Meg's face got red and her lips became tight. "Why? You know very well why, Alan. Because I washed the floor in here this morning. That's why."

Boots crossed the kitchen and put his front paws up on Meg's knees.

"Get down!" she cried, pushing the dog away from her. "Get out of here!"

"Here, Boots," Alan said. He put Boots out in the hall and then closed the kitchen door. He crossed the room and put a hand on Meg's shoulder. "Honey, I—"

Meg shook her husband's hand from her shoulder.

"You acted just now—when you told Boots to get out of here—you acted as if you were talking to me too," Alan said.

"Why don't you just go away, Alan, and leave me alone? Go waste your time painting more ugly pictures."

Alan could feel it coming. Meg was in another one of her moods. There was going to be another fight. He knew it. But he couldn't stop himself from saying, "I don't paint ugly pictures. I paint beautiful pictures."

"Not anymore, you don't!" Meg shot back at him. "I was in your studio this morning. I saw the painting you're working on. It's ugly, just like all the other ones you've painted lately. They all look as if they were painted by a crazy man. A man who doesn't know what he's doing."

"I just haven't been able to get the sky in the painting to look right yet. But I will."

"No you won't! If you ask me, you'll never sell another painting. The Stevens Gallery won't even hang your paintings anymore because they're so bad. So how will you ever be able to sell any of them?

And, if you can't sell your paintings, how will we live? How will we pay the rent? Buy food? They'll come and take out the telephone."

"Please, Meg, don't talk like that. I'm trying. I'm doing the best I can. But something seems to have gone wrong. When I paint these days it seems as if all the bad thoughts and feelings I've been having lately appear in my work."

Meg turned away.

Alan said, "I think my trouble has something to do with the way things are between us, Meg. It's hard for an artist to paint beautiful pictures when he feels so bad—so angry all the time."

"Are you trying to blame me for the bad work you've been doing lately?"

Alan shook his head. "No, I'm not. But I think I could do better work if things were all right between us, Meg. I'm sure I could. Oh, honey, we could be so happy again if only you wouldn't fight with me all the time. It seems we never have anything nice or kind to say to one another anymore."

"And I suppose that's my fault too?" Meg said, angrily.

"I don't know whose fault it is. I just wish we could stop fighting with each other all the time. I wish we could be the way we were when we were first married. We were happy then, Meg."

"Who could be happy with a husband who spends all his time painting pictures? Pictures that no one will buy, I might add."

"It's true that I haven't sold a painting in a while. But things will get better soon. I'll sell a painting—maybe more than one. I'm sure things are going to get better for me—for us."

"Well, I'm not so sure." Meg drank some of her coffee. "Would you mind leaving me alone, Alan? You've given me a headache. And when you go be sure to close the door behind you. I don't want your dirty dog coming in here again and making a mess of my clean kitchen."

"*Your* clean kitchen?" Alan yelled. "It's *my* kitchen too, Meg. Don't you forget that! I'll come into it whenever I want to! And Boots will also come in here, whenever *he* wants to!"

"Get out of my sight!" Meg screamed at him.

Alan stormed out of the kitchen and went back to his studio.

Once inside his studio, Alan took his palette knife and slashed the painting he had been working on into ribbons. The anger exploded inside him. He needed to paint. He needed to paint something that minute. He was going to paint. . . .

Meg, he thought. He lowered his head and covered his face with both hands. *Oh, Meg,* he thought, *what's wrong with us? What's happened to the love we once had for each other? When did it die? Why did it die?*

I hate her, he thought. *I hate Meg because she doesn't love me anymore. I know the trouble between us is partly my fault. I spend too much time painting—too much time away from her. I've been doing that for years. It's no wonder that we've drifted apart.*

Alan felt lost. And more angry than he had ever been in his life. Minutes later, he began to paint another picture. It was a picture of Meg sleeping in her bedroom.

His anger seemed to flow from his brain down into his arm and then into the picture he was painting. He painted a mosquito flying above the sleeping Meg. Then, he painted a second mosquito. He changed both mosquitoes to make them much larger than mosquitoes were in real life. He painted red marks on Meg's face

and arms where the mosquitoes were biting her. After he had done that, his anger
slowly went away and he began to feel
much better.

In the morning Alan was passing Meg's
bedroom, just as she was coming out. She
said, "I had a terrible dream last night. I
dreamed that I was being bitten by huge
mosquitoes. And they really hurt me."

Alan looked at the red marks on Meg's
face and arms. He thought about the picture of her that he had painted. He didn't
say anything.

"Oh, I don't know why I'm telling you
about my dream," she said as she walked
away from Alan. "You don't care about
my dreams—or about me either."

"That's not true, Meg. I do care. It's just
that I was thinking about—"

But she just kept walking down the hallway and then went downstairs.

Alan went into her bedroom and looked around. At first, he noticed nothing different about the room. But then he saw it. There, resting on Meg's pillow, was the largest mosquito he had ever seen. Feeling frightened, he quickly crossed the room and killed it. Then he returned to his studio.

Once there, he closed the door and stood in front of his easel thinking. *I painted mosquitoes biting Meg*, he thought. *She dreamed that she was being bitten by mosquitoes. And there was a large mosquito in her room just now.*

Could it be, he wondered, *that the mosquito in her room and the mosquitoes in my painting are in some way connected?*

He shook his head and smiled, knowing he was thinking silly thoughts. But then he got an idea. He began to paint a new picture. This one was also of Meg. In Alan's new painting, she was in a dark forest and it was raining very hard. Alan painted gray mud under her feet. Then he painted more mud so that it reached almost up to her knees. He painted Meg sinking down into the mud. He painted fear in her eyes, as she struggled to get out but couldn't get free.

Alan smiled, pleased with his work.

Later that day, when Meg awoke from her afternoon nap, Alan was waiting for her in the kitchen. "Did you have any bad dreams?" he asked her.

She gave him a strange look. "As a matter of fact, yes, I did have a bad dream during my nap. It was a terrible dream."

"Tell me about it."

"I dreamed that I was in a forest and it was raining very hard. The ground was very muddy. My feet got stuck in the mud and I began to sink down into it. I thought I was going to die. I screamed for help— and then I woke up."

Alan looked down at the shoes Meg was wearing. There was some mud on them. He felt a cold shiver run down his spine. *What have I done?* he thought. *These paintings seem to have come to life. I have to stop this craziness before I paint something that really harms Meg.*

He decided to tell Meg what he had been doing. Then he'd never paint another picture of her in danger again. After all, he was angry at her. But he didn't want to hurt her in any way.

"Meg, I want to tell you something."

When Alan had finished telling his wife about the two pictures he had painted, she looked at him for a minute and then said, "You're crazy, do you know that? You must be completely out of your mind to think that what you painted came to life."

"But there was a mosquito in your room after I painted that picture of mosquitoes biting you," he pointed out to her. "I saw it."

"It's summer," she replied. "Mosquitoes are everywhere during the summer and sometimes they get inside the house."

"When I painted you in the forest—

sinking down into the mud—Meg, there's mud on your shoes right now. Look at them."

Meg looked down at her shoes. "Before I went upstairs to take my nap, I was working outside in the garden. The ground was wet, so of course I got some mud on my shoes."

"Meg, I'm worried. I'm also frightened. I think something terrible might be about to happen to me—or to you. I—"

"You are the only terrible thing that has ever happened to me, Alan. You and that dirty dog of yours. I have to tell you the truth. I wish I'd never met you. I certainly wish I'd never married you."

Suddenly Alan had a bad feeling.

"Meg, where is Boots? I haven't seen him all day. Have you seen him?"

Meg smiled. "Yes, I have. I saw him—
for the last time—this morning. That was
when I took him to the dog pound."

"You did *what*?"

"That's right," she said, "your dog
won't be able to dirty my house ever
again. I told the man at the pound to
destroy him."

Alan was so angry he couldn't speak. He
ran from the kitchen and picked up the
telephone in the hall. He called the
pound, but it was too late. The man there
told him that Boots had been destroyed
that morning.

Tears filled Alan's eyes as he put down
the telephone. As he turned he saw Meg
standing in the kitchen doorway. She just
stared at him silently. Although he knew

he hated her at that moment, he couldn't feel anything. All he could think of was Boots, the dog he had loved so much, for so long. He ran down the hall and into his studio.

Alan awoke to find that he had fallen asleep in a chair in his studio. When he remembered what had happened, he began to cry.

He cried because his dog was dead, and he cried because the woman he had once loved had come to hate him. And he, in turn, had come to hate her.

He knew then that whatever love they

had once felt for one another was dead. He could no longer love someone who had found one of the worst possible ways to hurt him—by destroying Boots.

Suddenly something snapped in Alan's mind.

He promised himself that he would get even with Meg for what she had done to him. And he would do it the only way he knew.

He leaped to his feet, ran to his easel, and began to paint.

First he covered the empty canvas with gray paint. Then he began to paint a creature. It was not a man or a woman or an animal that he painted. It was something from the darkest part of Alan's soul.

He gave the creature orange eyes which seemed to shine with an evil light. He gave the creature two long hairy arms with large hands and sharp claws.

This painting, he thought, *will be my masterpiece. It will be the greatest painting I have ever done. When the world sees it, everyone will know that I'm a great painter, a better painter than the world has ever known.*

And Meg, she'll see that I'm a great painter too, he thought.

He began to laugh wildly. *Oh, yes*, he thought. *Meg will see my masterpiece. I know she will. She'll see it in her nightmares.*

He laughed even louder as he thought of how frightened Meg would be when the creature he was painting came to life in her dreams. He painted long dark hair all over the monster's body. *This will get even*

with her for what she did to Boots, he
thought, as he painted two more arms on
the creature, giving it four in all.

When he had finished the creature, he
stepped back from the easel and stared at
it.

He shivered in fear as he stared at the
creature's four long arms, its hairy body,
its wild orange eyes, its sharp claws.

The monster seemed about to leap off
the canvas and grab him.

Alan took another step backward and
drew a deep breath.

Then he went up to the easel again and
began to paint Meg sitting up in bed.
When he was finished, she sat with her
hands held up in front of her, her mouth
wide open and her eyes full of fear as she
stared up at the monster.

Alan changed the painting so that the creature's eyes were looking down at Meg. Minutes later, he put the finishing touches on his masterpiece. Then, as he was putting his brushes away, he heard a crash somewhere above him.

Alan looked at the clock on the wall of the studio. It was almost three o'clock in the morning. He listened, wondering if Meg had done something to cause the crash he had just heard. But he was sure she would be asleep at this late hour.

Just then he heard another crash upstairs. *Something's wrong*, he thought.

He ran out of the studio and up the stairs to the second floor.

Seconds later he heard strange sounds coming from inside Meg's bedroom. The sounds were not like anything he had ever heard before. He heard a growling and moaning, as if some *thing* were just waking up.

Inside the bedroom Meg screamed, and then something crashed to the floor.

Alan threw open the bedroom door and, in the moonlight coming through the bedroom windows, he saw it at the foot of the bed.

The creature.

The monster.

His masterpiece.

It was moving closer and closer toward

Meg, who was sitting up in her bed, frozen in fear. The creature put out an arm, and with its giant hand reached for Meg.

Alan, not able to move or speak, could only watch as the monster's big hand closed around Meg's throat. *This can't be happening*, he wanted to scream. But nothing came from his mouth. He stood there helplessly, as the creature tightened its grip on Meg's throat and squeezed and squeezed.

Alan ran up to the monster and tried to drag it away from the bed. It swung one of its large hairy arms and knocked him to the floor. He got to his feet and reached again for the creature, but he saw at once that it was too late.

Meg was dead. Her body lay across the

bed like a broken doll, all the life gone from it.

Alan cried out, and then hit the creature as hard as he could with both of his hands. It didn't move at all.

Then the monster turned to face its creator. And with one long sweep of its giant arm it reached for the man whose hate had given it life.